Kathy McKean
# MEDEA
After Euripides

# Salamander Street
PLAYS

## OTHER BOOKS BY KATHY McKEAN AVAILABLE FROM SALAMANDER STREET

### HEDDA GABLER

by Henrik Ibsen in a new version by Kathy McKean
ISBN: 9781919483221

Kathy McKean's new version of Ibsen's ***Hedda Gabler*** crackles with sharp contemporary speech and bruising humour. Returning from honeymoon to a mortgaged house and a stifling marriage, Hedda seethes for agency. Old rivals, failed courage and loaded pistols spiral towards catastrophe, exposing desire, control and fear in a world watching.

For my songbirds,
Sheena & Ossian

First published in 2026 by Salamander Street Ltd., a Wordville imprint. (info@salamanderstreetcom).

*Medea* © 2026 by Kathy McKean

All rights reserved.

All rights whatsoever in this play are strictly reserved and application for performance etc. should be made before rehearsals to Kathy McKean c/o Salamander Street. No performance may be given unless a license has been obtained. No rights in incidental music or songs contained in the work are hereby granted and performance rights for any performance/presentation whatsoever must be obtained from the respective copyright owners.

You may not copy, store, distribute, transmit, reproduce or otherwise make available this publication (or any part of it) in any form, or binding or by any means (print, electronic, digital, optical, mechanical, photocopying, recording or otherwise), without the prior written permission of the publisher. Any person who does any unauthorised act in relation to this publication may be liable to criminal prosecution and civil claims for damages.

All original production photography by Tommy Ga-Ken Wan

ISBN: 9781919483207

10 9 8 7 6 5 4 3 2 1

> Further copies of this publication can be purchased from
> www.salamanderstreet.com

# CONTENTS

Foreword by Nicole Cooper     iii

Introduction by Kathy McKean     ix

Director's Note by Gordon Barr     xi

Cast & Creative Team     xiv

MEDEA     1

Questions for Study and Discussion     58

Nicole Cooper as Medea (image: Twin City Pictures)

# FOREWORD

## PREPARATION:

When I began researching **Medea**, I came across details of the myth that stayed with me. In ***The Argonautica***, Apollonius of Rhodes describes how Medea becomes entangled in Jason's quest. Hera and Aphrodite, meddling in order to ensure Jason's success, persuade Kypris to enlist her son Eros. His task is simple: "shoot an arrow at the maiden and bewitch her with love for Jason." He agrees—not out of divine duty, but because his mother promises him a golden ball to play with.

And so, with the flick of a child god's hand, Medea's fate is sealed. Apollonius writes that *"a wearying pain scattered all prudent thoughts from her chest… a destructive love which crouched unobserved, burnt in Medea's heart."*

In an instant, she shifts from wary observer—suspicious of the Argonauts and protective of her family—to a young woman overwhelmed by a force she cannot name, let alone resist. For days, I kept returning to this moment. Perhaps because it echoes the love potion Oberon uses on Titania in ***A Midsummer Night's Dream***, I found myself wondering about the origins of the 'love potion' trope: the story of powerful beings toying with the hearts of mortals for their own gain or amusement.

I couldn't shake the thought that Medea, from the very beginning, was a pawn in a cruel game. Doomed to love a man beyond reason, beyond sense, beyond loyalty to her own family. Her love for Jason was not a choice. It was an affliction. A compulsion. A burden she could neither control nor extinguish. It drove her to commit unthinkable acts against her family and her people—acts that caused her anguish, confusion and a grief she could not articulate. Medea was not the cold-blooded harpy of later stories. She was a young woman caught in the web of a divine manipulation she never asked for.

This, for me, is the tragedy at the heart of ***Medea***. And in Kathy's writing, we were able—through rehearsal—to explore the boundaries of that love. There is a magnetic pull between Medea and Jason whenever they share the stage. The tension is electric: lust and seduction intertwined with pain and hatred. At any moment, Medea could give in, let him close, let him win—because she is compelled to put him first. Even after everything, she still loves him. And so the only escape is to destroy everything that binds them.

In Kathy's version of the play, Medea's struggle is not only with the final act she must commit, but with reclaiming the sovereignty of her own heart. Reclaiming her story. Reclaiming her destiny.

Her triumph at the end is not just vengeance. As she rises into the sky in the golden chariot sent by her grandfather, the sun, she unknowingly delivers a message to the gods themselves: they chose the wrong woman to toy with. And the devastation left in her wake is not hers alone to bear. Some of that blame belongs squarely at their feet.

None of this serves as an excuse for her behaviour, or an avenue to diminish the responsibility she has over her own actions. Medea understands, with devastating clarity, that the blood of her children will stain her hands for the rest of her life. She accepts that burden, adds it to the long list of wounds carved into her heart. But Medea also knows that Jason will forever carry a different wound: the knowledge that the love he exploited, betrayed and dismissed will be the very thing that haunts him and his legacy. Her actions will forever burn in his heart as Eros's arrow once burned in hers.

## PERFORMANCE:

There are a few moments from the first production of this play, at the Kibble Palace, that will stay with me forever: exploring, in

Greek, Medea's profound sense of otherness and weaving the fragile thread that bound her to the audience.

From our earliest conversations, all the way into rehearsals, Kathy and our director Gordon Barr were incredibly generous in encouraging me to lean into my Greek heritage as a way of illuminating Medea's otherness. We wanted her language to become both a shield and a weapon: something that could protect her from the audience's judgement, but also something she could wield to keep them at arm's length.

The Greek itself emerged through an entirely organic process. In rehearsal, there were moments when it simply felt natural to switch to Greek—when rage, grief or hatred surged so violently that Medea slipped instinctively into her mother tongue. It was as if her true self suddenly tore through the surface. She had always been too loud, too rash, too foreign for Jason. He had tried to reign her in, calm her storminess, dilute her culture to make it less embarrassing to him. Force her to fit in. With Jason's betrayal come permission to unleash her natural instincts, drop the façade.

What surprised me even more were the softer moments that called for Greek: the times she soothed her children, adored them, played with them. Speaking to them in that language felt like a reminder that although she had betrayed her family and homeland, they were never truly absent from her heart or mind. Her culture was a way of anchoring herself to the place she once belonged, even as she refused to assimilate into the world Jason had forced upon her. She wore her otherness like armour, letting Creon, Jason and even the audience underestimate her. Sometimes I would translate the line in my next sentence to allow the audience in, other times I would purposefully leave them in the dark. If they didn't understand that was not my problem. That distance, that refusal to soften or translate herself, became part of her power. It reminded everyone watching that Medea is not simply a woman displaced; she is a woman who remembers exactly where she comes from, and who she once was, even as the world around her tries to reshape her into something else.

One of the most striking elements of Kathy's reimagining was the removal of the chorus as a physical presence. In our traverse staging—with the action unfolding only a few feet from the audience—we understood early on that the chorus would not disappear, but transform. Its role would be taken up by the people seated around us. Medea's confidantes, witnesses, judges and silent companions would be the very people who had come to watch her unravel. It was to them she would plead, to them she would confess, to them she would break.

We knew this in theory. But it wasn't until the performances began that I understood the true weight of that relationship—and the fragile boundaries that held it together. I could see the faces of the women in the audience as I warned them, "this could happen to you." I could feel their warmth when I met their gaze, silently begging for help each time Jason entered Medea's orbit. I had underestimated how intimate that bond would become, how quickly a sense of community would form between us. And I had not anticipated how violently that bond would rupture when Medea took those final, dreadful steps toward her children's bedroom. Every night, I felt the audience recoil—a collective flinch, a breath held in disbelief.

Losing their support was painful, but it also ignited something in Medea. The audience's silence—once a source of solace—became a reckoning. Their horror at her actions became the mirror in which she recognised the brutal truth: she no longer belongs among them. The women whose eyes had been an anchor for Medea could not follow her into the realm she was about to enter. In that moment, she stepped beyond their judgement, beyond their comprehension, into the terrible, transcendent freedom that only one with the blood of the gods running through their veins could harness.

## POST-SHOW:

The most beautiful thing about Kathy's writing is its accessibility. She has this astonishing ability to compress entire paragraphs of emotional depth into a handful of precise, devastating phrases. The language feels epic in scope, yet somehow still intimate—as if she's whispering directly into your ear while invoking the weight of myth. Performing this play was an emotional gauntlet. Every night I left the stage utterly spent, exhilarated and trembling with adrenaline, still vibrating with the aftershock of that horrific act of violence.

And every night, without fail, Isabelle Joss—who played the Nurse—would pass by my dressing room just to check in. She understood how gruelling the journey through the material was, how much it demanded. She always knew exactly what I needed, mirroring the tenderness and intuition of the Nurse and Medea's relationship. Sometimes it was a smile and a long exhale. Other times it was a wordless hug. Those moments grounded me.

I remember watching an interview with Helen McCrory about her preparation for ***Medea*** at the National. She spoke about having to invent a whole new way of acting—as a parent—in order to access Medea's journey. I noted it at the time, but I didn't truly understand what she meant.

And then I played her. And I understood.

Medea's pain is unbearable. Literally. She does what she does because, in her world, there is no other option. To kill her beautiful children, she must become someone else—something else—a being forged out of betrayal, exile and divine manipulation. As an actor and a mother, I had to draw a hard, immovable line between myself and the character. Normally I lean into my lived experience to find truth and authenticity, but with Medea I couldn't even begin to imagine myself in her place. So I didn't. I surrendered to Kathy's writing and to the scale of Medea's myth.

The world she inhabits—Jason and the Argonauts, the golden fleece, the long journey to Corinth—all of it helped me build a reality that existed on another plane entirely. Her life before the play even begins is so vast, so extreme, that it dwarfs anything I could personally compare it to. Sometimes a character simply takes over, and as an actor you have to let them in, follow them from the first line to their last, and trust that you'll find your way back.

And then you exhale in your dressing room. And maybe—if you're lucky—you get a hug.

**Nicole Cooper**
2026

# INTRODUCTION

There are so many versions and adaptations of *Medea* already in existence. The reasons for this one are Nicole Cooper and Gordon Barr—they needed a version for the Kibble Palace in Glasgow's Botanic Gardens for a small cast to give them the possibility of expanding the incredible work they have always done in the company. Nicole was performing Hamlet and Gordon worried what to give her next and was considering the Greeks; I had just listened to a podcast about *Medea* which made me want to look at the play anew and we went from there. It is strange now to reflect on the anxieties we had around the departure it represented for Bard in the Botanics and how it might be received: Gordon worried about the distance from Shakespeare; Nicole worried about how contemporary the language was; I worried. And I have notebooks full of those worries that is also called research. It is, however, a gift to a playwright to know who one is writing a role for and I had witnessed already the impact Nicole has on an audience, how immediately empathetic we feel towards her, her fearlessness, her instincts, her fierce and focussed intellect and how deeply and immediately she engages with the humanity of the characters she plays.

In terms of approaching the adaptation, a lot of my decisions were led by practical considerations. The adaptation was always for the Kibble Palace and so a chorus of performers was never a possibility but the intimacy of the venue suggested early on how the audience might function in their place. My first draft had children in it—I came across so many references in my research to the power of having them in the production—but we agreed that I'd attempt one without them and again, I looked to make them present for Medea in other ways. A fiery chariot not being within the budget, the first part of the play that I wrote was the Nurse's speech at the end which helped set the tone and rhythm of the script for me, although what Isabelle Joss achieved with it went beyond what I could have hoped for.

What makes ***Medea*** relevant now are the aspects of the play that have always made it relevant: how we other and monster difference (in the immediate context in which I was writing, the rejection and displacement felt by so many in the aftermath of the Brexit vote, the difference in our response to refugees from Ukraine and those fleeing other conflicts and disasters); the injustice in the silencing and misrepresentation of voice and self; and the rage there is at being being victimised or positioned as a victim; the pressure to be always just a little bit less or a little bit more. The idea of rage is something currently being reexamined and repositioned across much critical and creative discourse, particularly as it relates to those who have been silenced or expected to adapt, assimilate or conform. There's also the immediate subject matter of the action: the ways in which love and hate become obsessive and destructive; the devastation of humiliation and despair; vengeance as a force that can only destroy.

The action at the end makes sense to Medea as the only course of action open to her: the only way for her to defeat Jason is to bring a greater devastation on herself. We see this in her agonising throughout the play—it's important that we don't see this at the end. We are not operating in a moral universe we recognise. There is no condemnation of Medea in Euripides—she is triumphant and terrifying and entirely herself in all the ways that others have tried to destroy and deny.

**Kathy McKean**
2026

# DIRECTOR'S NOTE

In 2019, I directed a production of *Hamlet* for Bard in the Botanics (the company of which I am Artistic Director) with Nicole Cooper giving an incredible performance in the title role. This was the latest in a series of collaborations between Nicole and myself that had previously seen her play a number of Shakespeare's leading roles—including, amongst others, Cleopatra, Isabella, Lady Macbeth, Rosalind and Coriolanus.

I was keen to find a new challenge for this extraordinary performer and, one night, I was sat with Kathy McKean discussing future possibilities. Until that point, Bard in the Botanics had focused almost exclusively on Shakespeare. But as we talked, the idea of Nicole playing Medea was raised and instantly seemed irresistible.

Having been a great admirer of Kathy's writing for many years—and then discovering that she had recently and coincidentally been looking into Medea's story—it felt, in a very 'Greek' way, that the fates were colliding and so Bard in the Botanics' first commissioned script was born. Kathy would write a new version of ***Medea***, inspired by Euripides' original, with Nicole playing the iconic character.

Now I must confess something. I have always loved the stories and characters of Greek tragedy—but I've often struggled with the formality of their texts. So I set Kathy the challenge of creating a script for ***Medea*** which would honour the epic storytelling of Euripides but would also humanise these characters for a modern audience—something which would allow them to really interact rather than deliver set speeches at each other.

A little while later, Kathy read me the first piece of text she had written—actually the final speech of the play— to see if she was on the right track. It is no exaggeration to say that I wept at its beauty, its poetry and its humanity. From just this one fragment of writing, I knew that Kathy was creating something very special.

The production was delayed due to the pandemic but Kathy continued to work on the text and allowed both myself and Nicole to input our thoughts at each stage. Nicole's own identity (Greek-Zambian) influenced the development of the character—as did both Kathy and Nicole's experiences as mothers. Each new draft refined and clarified Kathy's unique vision of Medea—an outsider feared by the new society in which she finds herself; a powerful demigod struggling with human frailties; an extraordinary woman silenced and erased from the narrative by a gaslighting husband; a fiercely devoted and loving mother willing to make a terrifying sacrifice to reclaim her own identity.

Each of the many facets of this complex and fascinating character sprang sharply into life in Kathy's text and in Nicole's performance, supported by a phenomenally talented cast—Johnny Panchaud (Jason), Isabelle Joss (Nurse) and Alan Steele (Creon / Tutor).

Despite the complexity and emotional intensity of the story, the rehearsal process was one of the smoothest, most enjoyable and most exciting I have experienced in 25 years of directing. Each day brought new discoveries by a team inspired by Euripides' original and, especially, by Kathy's remarkable new version which seamlessly blends the classic and the contemporary. It was a very special process that created a very special production of a very special script and it will forever be a piece of work that I am incredibly proud to have been a part of.

**Gordon Barr**
2026

Nicole Cooper as Medea (photo: by Tommy Ga-Ken Wan)

Alan Steele as Creon (photo: by Tommy Ga-Ken Wan)

*Medea* was first performed by Bard in the Botanics in the Kibble Palace, Glasgow on 24th June 2022. The cast was as follows:

| | |
|---|---|
| **MEDEA:** | **Nicole Cooper** |
| **JASON:** | **Johnny Panchaud** |
| **NURSE:** | **Isabelle Joss** |
| **TUTOR/CREON:** | **Alan Steele** |
| | |
| **WRITER:** | **Kathy McKean** |
| **DIRECTOR/DESIGNER:** | **Gordon Barr** |
| **ASSISTANT DIRECTOR/SCRIPT CONSULTANT:** | **Colette Hamiliton** |
| **WARDROBE:** | **Carys Hobbs** |
| **PRODUCTION MANAGER:** | **Tom Saunders** |
| **STAGE MANAGER:** | **Suzie Goldberg** |
| **COSTUME SUPERVISOR:** | **Rosaleen D. Orr** |

# CAST & CREATIVE TEAM

## Nicole Cooper | Medea

Nicole is from Zambia and Greece and trained in Scotland at RCS (RSAMD). Nicole is an Associate Artist with Bard in the Botanics.

Theatre credits include: *Cinderella: A fairytale* (Lyceum Theatre, Edinburgh); *Our Brother* (A Play, A Pie & A Pint); (Singapore festival of the Arts, Lemon Tree, and Traverse Theatre); *A View From the Bridge* (Tron Theatre, Glasgow); *Hedda Gabler* (Bard in the Botanics); *Macbeth* (An Undoing) (Rose Theatre, Kingston; Theatre for a New Audience, New York; Lyceum Theatre, Edinburgh); *Lear's Fool* (Bard in the Botanics); *Macbeth* (An Undoing) (Lyceum Theatre, Edinburgh); *The Spark* (A Play, A Pie & A Pint); *Medea* (Bard in the Botanics); *The Tempest* (Tron Theatre); *The Winter's Tale, Twelfth Night, Hamlet, As You Like It* (all Bard in the Botanics); *Sleeping Beauty* (The Byre Theatre); *Much Ado About Nothing, Antony and Cleopatra* (both Bard in the Botanics); *How to Fix a Broken Wing* (Catherine Wheels Theatre Company); *Pleading* (A Play, A Pie & A Pint); *Scribble* (Scribble Play); *Timon of Athens, Measure for Measure, Coriolanus,*
*Macbeth* (all Bard in the Botanics); *Sleeping Beauty* (PACE); *Love's Labours Lost, The Merchant of Venice* (both Bard in the Botanics); *Horizontal Collaboration* (Fire Exit); *The Comedy of Errors, Julius Caesar, Othello, As You Like It, The Tempest, A Midsummer Night's Dream, Hamlet, King Lear, Twelfth Night, Richard III* (all Bard in the Botanics)

Film and television credits include: *Getting Close* (National Theatre of Scotland); *Where Did He Go?* (Traverse Theatre); *The Nest* (Studio Lambert); *The Novels That Shaped Us* (IWC Media); *Jonathan Creek* (BBC); *Fried* (Bwark Productions)

Awards: Nominations for Best Performance as Hamlet, Lady Macbeth, Lear's Fool, Hedda Gabler (Critics' Awards For Theatre in Scotland); Nominated for Best Performance as Lady Macbeth

(Drama Desk Awards, NY); Winner of Best Performance as Coriolanus, Medea (Critics' Awards For Theatre in Scotland)

## Johnny Panchaud | Jason

Johnny is a Glasgow-based actor and graduate of The Royal Welsh College of Music & Drama. His theatre credits include: Soldier/Gaveston understudy in *Edward II* (The National Theatre), *The Gentleman in The Lower Depths* (The Richard Burton Company), Lopakhin in *The Cherry Orchard* (The Richard Burton Company), James in *The Spark* (Play Pie & Pint), Jason in *Medea* (Bard In The Botanics). Hotspur in *Henry IV* (Bard In The Botanics) and Rochester in *Jane Eyre* (Bard In The Botanics).

Johnny's TV and film credits include: *Shetland* (BBC), *Skinjacker* (Zoghogg Productions), *Polly Baggage* (BFI) and *Handle With Care* (New Lore).

## Isabelle Joss | Nurse

Izzi trained at The Royal Conservatoire of Scotland and has worked extensively as an actor in theatre, TV, film and radio throughout Scotland, the UK, and internationally. Izzi won the Pitlochry Festival Theatre's prestigious Leon Sinden award for Best Supporting Actress for *Good Things* by Liz Lochead.

Izzi's recent theatre credits includes *Aladdin, Hedda Gabbler* (CATS award winner for Best Production), *Merry Wives of Wishaw, Medea* (CATS award winner for Best Production), *Much Ado About Nothing* for Bard in the Botanics; *Peter Gynt, Men Should Weep* at the National Theatre in London; *Martha, The Voice Thief, The Story of the Little Gentleman, Lifeboat* (West End, Broadway, Australian and New Zealand tour) for Catherine Wheels Theatre Company; *Hauns Aff My Haunted Bin, Digital Detox, Rachel's Cousin, Faster Louder, Take Me If You Need Me, I Heart Maths, Just The Job* at Oran Mor's Play, Pie & A Pint; *Faithful Ruslan–The Story Of A Guard Dog (*Co Production with Belgrade & Citizen's Theatre);

*Jack and the Beanstalk, Cinderella, Sinbad (*Websters Memorial Theatre); *The Pokey Hat (*Grinagog Theatre); Breaker (Underbelly); *Great Expectations* for Richard Stoneman (UK tour and the West End); *Scrooge* (The Cottiers Theatre); *Entartet* (Vanishing Point); *Sub Rosa* (Fringe First Winner, Fire Exit Theatre Company); *Steel Magnolias, Shining Souls* (CATs award winner, The Tron Theatre); *Good Things, The Prime Of Miss Jean Brodie, The Servant 'O Twa Maisters, The Life Of Stuff* (Pitlochry Festival Theatre); *Hansel & Gretel, The Selfish Giant, The Big Funk (*The Arches Theatre); *Gilt* (7:84); *Uncle Vanya (*UK & US tour with Theatre Babel); *The Reel Of The Hanged Man* (Stellar Quines).

TV includes *Shetland, Lovesick, Silent Witness, Life of Riley, Dear Green Place, Taggart, The Bill, Kitchen, Feel the Force*, and *Goth*.

Film includes P*ale Star, American Cousins, Small Faces, The Acid House.*

Radio: *The Breach, The Tragic History of my Nose, Kidnapped, Iona, Whoever You Choose to Love, Love for Lydia, Forever Young, For the Love of Willie.*

## Alan Steele | Tutor/Creon

Alan's credits for Bard in the Botanics include Sir John Falstaff in *Henry IV* and Prospero in *The Tempest* (both performances earning him a CATS Award nomination for Outstanding Performance), Bottom in *A Midsummer Night's Dream*, Lady Bracknell in *The Importance of Being Earnest*, Malvolio in *Twelfth Night* and roles in *Medea, Jane Eyre, The WInter's Tale, Hamlet, As You Like It, Coriolanus* and *Love's Labours Lost*, as well as reprising the role of Falstaff last summer in *The Merry Wives of Wishaw*. He has been the Dame for multiple Christmas seasons at the Byre Theatre in St Andrews. Alan's other theatre credits include several seasons at Pitlochry Festival Theatre with appearances in, amongst others, Rona Munro's *The Last Witch, Travesties, Europe* and *Good Things* (Leon Sinden Award); Peter Arnott's *Unspotted Snow* (Mull Theatre Scottish tour); the title role in *Dracula* (Courtyard, Hereford); the one man show *Backstage at the Pussycat Club* (The Arches, Glasgow); *A Taste of Honey* and *The Crucible* (Tag / NTS). He has toured the Highlands and Islands in many shows including *The Weir* and *The Lonesome West* and played the title role in *Macbeth* with Mull Theatre. He played Gil Martin the devil in a highly acclaimed production of *Confessions of Justified Sinner* (Rowan Tree) and on BBC Radio 4. His TV credits include the title role of John Knox in the BBC's *The Sword and The Cross*.

## Kathy McKean | Writer

Kathy is a graduate of the University of Glasgow Theatre Studies, English and Creative Writing programmes. Recent work includes *Getting Close,* written as part of the National Theatre of Scotland's Scenes for Survival Project, directed by Nick Bone, T*he Present Tense*, directed by Colette Hamilton and written with support from the Playwrights' Studio Scotland and Magnetic North's Rough Mix programme, *The Spark* for A Play, A Pie and A Pint, and a new version of *Hedda Gabler*, also directed by Gordon Barr. *Medea* and *Hedda Gabler* both won the Best Production Award at the CATS (2022 & 2025). She is currently developing work with composer Ben Fletcher with support from Magnetic North.

## Gordon Barr | Director

Gordon has been Artistic Director of Bard in the Botanics for over two decades, directing and producing more than 100 productions in that time. His own directing credits for the company include *Hedda Gabler* (CATS Award for Best Production, CATS nomination for Best Director), T*he Importance of Being Earnest, Medea* (CATS Award for Best Production; CATS nomination for Best Director) and more than 20 of Shakespeare's plays including, most recently, *A Midsummer Night's Dream, Romeo and Juliet, The Merry Wives of Wishaw, Henry IV, Much Ado About Nothing,*

*The Winter's Tale, Twelfth Night, As You Like It* and *Hamlet*. He has written and directed the Byre Theatre / Bard in the Botanics panto for the past decade, with recent titles including *Aladdin, Beauty & the Beast, Cinderella, Snow White* and *Mother Goose*. He has taught Shakespeare extensively, including a number of productions for the Royal Conservatoire of Scotland, and has worked on projects for a variety of companies across Scotland including NTS, Macrobert, Cumbernauld Theatre, TAG and 7:84.

## Colette Hamilton | Assistant Director/Script Consultant

Colette is a director from San Diego, California. She holds an MFA in Classical Contemporary Text Directing from the Royal Conservatoire of Scotland and an honours BA in Theatre Arts from University of California San Diego.

Directing credits include: *How Not to Fund a Honeymoon* (Edinburgh Fringe Festival/Very Rascals); *Freezer Cake* (Brighton Fringe Festival; The Libra Cafe, London); *The Present Tense* (Emergence Festival 2023); *Fill Fill Fill Fill Fill Fill Fill* (RCS), *Medea* (Assistant Director, Bard in the Botanics); *The Spark* (Assistant Director, A Play A Pie & A Pint); *Fefu and Her Friends, Rumours* (UCSD); *RockPaperWORLD* (Scripps Ranch Theatre); *The Last 5 Years* (Assistant Director, Cygnet Theatre).

## Carys Hobbs | Wardrobe

Carys trained in Costume Design at QMU, Edinburgh. Some recent designs include; *Moorcroft* (Tron Theatre); Design mentor for CATS Best production winner *Hedda Gabler* and 2022 winner *Medea, Henry IV* and *Jekyll and Hyde* for Bard in the Botanics, *Walking Tall Tales* events (Tron Theatre Education), *The Dutch Courtesan* (RCS).

Carys has been the Head of Design for Bard in the Botanics since 2014 with some of her favourite designs including *Much Ado About Nothing, Antony & Cleopatra, Measure for Measure, Taming of the Shrew, Coriolanus, Dr Faustus, Romeo and Juliet* and *Merchant of Venice*.

Other credits also include *Bingo!* (Stella Quines & Grid Iron). *Coriolanus Vanishes* (Fire Exit), *Last Tango in Partick* (NTS and CRUDE with Grid Iron), *GlasGlow* (Itison). For Tron Theatre: *Shall Roger Casement Hang?, Colquhoun &Macbryde, Happy Days and Brothers Karamazov*. She has also been the designer of the Byre Pantomime since 2017.

## Bard in the Botanics | Producer

Bard in the Botanics is Scotland's biggest and best-loved classical theatre company, renowned for its innovative and accessible productions. Its annual programme of work is centred around a summer season of classic plays staged in the beautiful surroundings of Glasgow's Botanic Gardens. Since its inception in 2001, the company has staged more than 120 productions, primarily Shakespeare, having tackled more than 30 of his titles. The company has also produced work by other Renaissance playwrights, including Christopher Marlowe, John Webster and John Fletcher. In recent years, the company has expanded its remit to incorporate other classical plays and stories, often in new versions by contemporary Scottish playwrights. These titles include, amongst others: *Medea; Hedda Gabler; Jekyll & Hyde* and *Sherlock Holmes: A Scandal in Bohemia*. In addition to the company's classical work, it also co-produces and creates the annual panto for the Byre Theatre, St Andrews.

Johnny Paunchaud as Jason & Nicole Cooper as Medea
(photo: by Tommy Ga-Ken Wan)

Kathy McKean

# **MEDEA**

After Euripides

## CHARACTERS

**NURSE**
**TUTOR**
**MEDEA**
**JASON**
**CREON**

## SETTING

A space between

## A NOTE ON THE TEXT

Words in [ ] indicate the unspoken completion of the character's thought.

/ indicates the point at which a character is interrupted.

A blank space after a character's name indicates a non-verbal exchange.

In the original production, where Medea's speech is italicised, the lines were spoken in Greek and/or English; when underlined, in Greek only. This may be adopted or adapted freely.

**NURSE:** This is not a love story
This is not a story of love
Maybe they two were the world's greatest lovers
Who cares
You maybe
No' me
I care they didnae keep it a'tween themselves where these things should be kept
He couldnae anyway
I wish to God he'd never placed one foot in that ship
That as a child he'd stepped on a boat that had rocked and tipped and put him into the water and everybody had a big laugh and the story I'd be telling you now would be of a boy who never went near the water again because he couldnae take a joke because he couldnae stand it when folk laughed at him
I wish that the gods had never put that idea in his head
Nor men
That what he had had been enough for him
At some point
At any point
Enough
And I know you'll look at her and you'll think she's the problem
Then deny it
Because she's a bit [other]
And you're not [xenophobic]
Of course not
But she's not
Quite [the same as us]
And we're a very friendly people
Everyone says so
So if she's had a problem fitting in wi' us well

That's on her
No one asked her to come here
They say he was questing for a kingdom
Her man
As was
Jason
A kingdom, so they say
Or the skin of an animal
It doesnae matter
The reason is always the same:
The horizon he could see was never enough for him
He had to sail on
So his name would live on
So he took his fleece
He took his golden treasure
And he took her
Because he could
And her
Yes, it's true what they say
She is clever
And yes, she has a power that is to be feared
But clever as she is
She was stupid enough to believe him when he told her her home was with him
And powerful as she is
She was weak enough to believe that the promises he made he would only ever speak to her
And maybe she was right to believe him
Maybe in the moment he spoke those vows he meant them
But words are one thing
And life is another
And he saw his dream dying

His name fading
And the chance for something new

She's twenty-two
His something new
And she believes him
She believes that the words only count when they're spoken to her and when they're spoken here
No' in some far off place
To far off people
Or to children who belong neither here
Nor there
And she's not the only one
So we're all celebrating
Oh, we're all delighted
They just look like they belong
Time to move on
Time for new stories
With more future in them than past

But the past is still with us
Howling to be heard
And they've forgotten, maybe, about what she has done for Jason
That for love of him she fought monsters
For love of him she killed kings
And they are wrong to forget that, I think

*TUTOR enters carrying books for the boys*

**TUTOR:** Where are the boys?

**NURSE:** Playing
    Away fae here

*MEDEA howls*

**NURSE:** Aye
Away fae here

**TUTOR:** She's still /

**NURSE:** Aye

**TUTOR:** Have you slept?

**NURSE:** No

**TUTOR:** Have you spoken to her?

**NURSE:** No
She's grieving for a man still living
I cannae go near her 'til

**TUTOR:** 'Til what?

**NURSE:** I don't know
I was gonnae say, until it stops

*MEDEA howls*

But it won't stop
Will it?

**TUTOR:** She has to eat

**NURSE:** What?

**TUTOR:** To keep going. She has to eat.

**NURSE:** Okay

**TUTOR:** So she'll have to stop. Or not. And then that will stop her so either way

**NURSE:** Really? Is that it?

**TUTOR:** Yes
No
Where are the boys?

**NURSE:** They're fine
They're not fine but

**TUTOR:** It's not fine

**NURSE:** No

**TUTOR:** No, I mean it's worse than not fine.
The king he's issued orders
He wants them gone.

**NURSE:** Medea?

**TUTOR:** Yes

**NURSE:** Not the boys?

**TUTOR:** Yes

**NURSE:** Is it Jason?
Is this his doing?

**TUTOR:** Maybe. I only heard it was the king

**NURSE:** But
No
They can't do this
They can't just

**TUTOR:** We don't have to go with her

**NURSE:**

**TUTOR:** She's done herself no favours.
She never does.
Creon's heard what she's been saying.
How could he not?

**NURSE:** No.
   Jason wouldn't.
   Not to his sons.

**TUTOR:** You can't tell her.

**NURSE:** He's their father. They need him.

**TUTOR:** He doesn't need them.
   He's a new wife.
   A real wife not /

**NURSE:** They're his blood

**TUTOR:** Half of it. He's not the first man to leave / [a woman]

**NURSE:** He's the first for her. This will end her. He / can't

**TUTOR:** He can do what he likes now. She can't touch him

**NURSE:** And the boys?
   What about them?

**TUTOR:** I know. But it is Creon's right

**NURSE:** It's wrong
   She'll not go near them, you know.
   There's too much of him in them.
   Jason is all she can see.

*MEDEA cries out*

**TUTOR:**

**NURSE:**

**TUTOR:** They're saying she chopped her brother to pieces. Threw the parts into the sea.

**NURSE:** Aye.
   That's what they're saying

**TUTOR**: I think Creon's quite keen his daughter's new husband stays whole

**NURSE**: If I had the strength in my hands I would tear him apart myself for what he's done to her

**TUTOR**:

**NURSE**: What?
Is that wrong?

**TUTOR**: They were never married.
Not really.

**NURSE**: And the boys, they're not really his sons?

**TUTOR**:

**NURSE**: Then you're as bad as him

**TUTOR**: He's a man. And one day he may even be king.

**NURSE**: And her?
What is she?

*MEDEA enters.*

**TUTOR**: Without him? She's just a woman who doesn't know when to keep her mouth shut.

*They leave; the books remain on stage.*

**MEDEA**: *I know what you say about me*
I see every look
I hear every word
I know I know I know I have never been one of you
But I stand here before you
A woman
Forced to speak against the sea of your accusations

To tell you that I am just
That you know me
You know my fate
As I know yours
I gave everything
To be left with nothing
And you know how that feels
If you don't, I pity you
Because this will happen to you
You who sit and hold hands and make love look so easy
I'm so sorry
But this is coming for you
It is not a fight you will ever win
And yet
And still
And still you will give everything to be with him because you have found your reason for life
To say at the end: I spent it with him
And somehow you don't notice that he gives up nothing
You must sacrifice home
Because his life is not there
And your life is with him
Friends, because
Dreams, because
Your world becomes smaller
Your world becomes him
And always his world is bigger
If he is unhappy, he can find new lands, sail new seas, find new loves
He can leave you
But you have had his children
Their pain is yours
Not even in death can you leave him

I have heard people say that there is safety in this
Protected by walls and help with the washing and everything being better than it ever was before
Men face danger
When war comes they must go and fight while we remain safely at home
Safely at home
If you think home is a safe place for a woman then you have not been paying attention
I would rather stand three times on the front line of a battle than give birth to a single child
There death would come faster and more painlessly to me
Better to die a hero and be remembered with honour than die soaked in my own blood, my life forgotten, my death a nothing, a secret, a shame
Our bodies are disposable and so are our lives
These are all the lessons my marriage has taught me
At night he holds my heart out in front of me still beating
The blood pumping down to his elbow through the knuckles on his hand
We watch together as it pools at our feet on the ground
There is no pain a man can invent in battle that he has not already inflicted on me
Better dead than unwanted
Better dead than alone
And you think you are not alone
But you will be
Just not as alone as me
*I am a stranger in a strange land and I know how strange you find me*
*Your eyes are the shadow that always follow me*
He has taken everything from me

*CREON enters*

**CREON:** Medea
I thought you'd be out here
Howling at the wind

**MEDEA:** Howling?
Am I a wild animal? Is that what you think, Creon?
I weep
That is all
Is that not to be expected of me?

**CREON:** Save your tears, Medea.
And your lies
I know what you are

**MEDEA:** I am your daughter's husband's wife.
That is all you know about me.

**CREON:** Out of respect /

**MEDEA:** What respect do you show / me

**CREON:** Out of respect I have come to tell you my decision in person. You're not a citizen here and your only right to remain came through your

**MEDEA:** My husband?

**CREON:** Jason.
Through your association with Jason. You no longer have his protection and it has been decided that you and your children must leave.

**MEDEA:**

**CREON:** Now.
Medea.
And I will watch you go
Those that come after me won't use words

**MEDEA:** No
   No
   You cannot mean [it]
   You know what that would [mean]
   Why we came here
   How can you [do this to me]
   What have I ever done to you?

**CREON:** I am not a stupid man and I thought you were a clever woman. I don't listen to rumour, Medea, but you have been stupid with your threats. I will protect my daughter against any harm. Whatever dark thoughts you have, whatever revenge you seek, you can do it from where we don't have to listen to the evil you speak.

**MEDEA:** The evil?
   Evil?
   I know what people here see when they look at me
   I am enough alike and not alike to make them afraid
   But not you, Creon
   Not you
   You say you don't listen to rumour
   So you, of everyone
   You can see me
   You can see that whatever weapons I may make of my words, that's all they are
   Words
   They are all that is left to me and I have never
   Never
   I have never directed them against you or your daughter
   How can I?
   You have shown me only kindness and she is blameless in this
   It is her new husband who has [wronged me]

But there is nothing I can do but howl
And hear that sound echo back to me
And if you tell me to be silent, you have the power to silence me
But not this!
Please
Let me stay
Please
If you want to see me broken, here I am
Here I am
I have no power
The only strength that exists here between us is yours

**CREON**: Your words are not powerless
You are nothing to me
My daughter is everything
It's time for you to go

**MEDEA**: Think of me for one moment as your child

**CREON**: You disgust me
I know what you did to your father
You betrayed him and stole from him for a stranger

**MEDEA**: I loved my father
I loved Jason more

**CREON**: What you call love turns so quickly to something dark in you. Is it true that you killed your own brother to escape the punishment you deserved?

**MEDEA:** Please
Please
No one can give me back the land I love
The family I
Lost

Just give me the chance to just stay here in this land that I know

**CREON:** No

*MEDEA kneels*

**CREON:** No.
They're coming, Medea
You had better be ready to go

**MEDEA:** One day

**CREON:** No

**MEDEA:** One day
Let me leave without
Without
Let me speak to my boys
Let me tell them it's for the best
Let me tell them of your kindness
One day
We'll leave
I promise
We'll be gone

**CREON:** One day?

**MEDEA:** Whatever you think of me
Think of them
One day
What can I do in a day?
I am alone
Abandoned by a man who feels no shame, no pity
Surrounded by strangers
I am helpless

I have no weapons, no armies, no palaces, nothing to defend me
Except you

**CREON**: I will be merciful but do not mistake kindness for weakness
If you or your children are here to pollute another sunrise their blood will be on your hands
Not mine
One day
That is all

**MEDEA**: That's all I need

*CREON leaves.*

*MEDEA rises.*

That's all I need.

*Did you see this?*
*Did you see me?*
On my knees before this
This
To beg for
When I have stood far above where he stands

In my father's palace there were springs that bubbled with milk and perfume and wine
In this land everything is dirty. Nothing is sacred. Nothing here is divine
I am a god to be worshipped and I have been on my knees before
I will humiliate myself no more

Oh I want to cleanse the past out of my mind
Make my vision clear
Still still still it would live on in his
This shared story he can tell and shape in his own way
I will cut it out of him

Tear down that statue
Smash it to pieces
Use the broken pieces to build my image there
Because I am not what others say about me
I am myself
I am what I have always been
I have always been here breaking through those false gods of womanhood you worship
Submitting silently to their suffering
Adored in their wordless distress
No more of this
I have a right to be heard
We are nothing
Without cracks
And through the cracks I am screaming:
I will have my revenge
And when I do, I will not accept the judgement of a single one of you
There are no crossroads here
There is only one path that is open in front of me
You may stand with me but you will not stand in my way

I was born in fire
And I will burn their world to the ground
There will be no more silence
Not from me
Until I have heard them scream

One day
Don't look up, Creon
I'm bringing the sky down on you
One day
That is all
It's enough

*JASON enters. Perhaps he has been watching her.*

**JASON:** Oh Medea.

**MEDEA:** You

**JASON:** All you needed to be was quiet.
You do know that, don't you?

The one thing you can never be and yet I hoped
For the sake of the boys
I had hoped

**MEDEA:** What did you hope?

**JASON:** I had hoped that you would put them first
Put their needs before your own
I don't care about the things you have called me
I forgive you
I know you'll say you don't ask for my forgiveness but that's okay
I forgive you anyway
I know
That you cannot help yourself
You speak as you were taught to speak
You cannot escape what you were born into and so I suppose
I cannot blame you for that but I had hoped
I had hoped you had been here long enough, been around me long enough, to learn how people here expect you to behave

You are a guest here
And instead of showing gratitude, you make threats against them!

**MEDEA**: Why are you here?

**JASON**: I know you hate me but I could never hate you. We have been through so much together. And the boys. I have means now. I will not see you without the things you need.

**MEDEA**: You coward

**JASON**: I wish only good things for you

**MEDEA**: You can look me in the eye and say that?

**JASON**: I can
I mean it
I can

**MEDEA**: Of course you can
Of all the things you have told me you mean
Of all the things you've sworn on your life to be true, why not this?

**JASON**: I meant those things too

**MEDEA**: Liar

**JASON**: I do love you.

**MEDEA**: Liar

**JASON**: You see
This
This is what you have done
You could have had a home here
You could have had a life here
With me

If only you could have quieted that rage that lives / inside you

MEDEA: That rage?
That rage?
Was it rage that saved your life when you came to steal from my father?
You had another name for it then

JASON: Ah, yes, I have heard that now you claim my victories as your own

MEDEA: Your victories?
What victories did you win?
You who assembled the greatest, the strongest of men to quest for the golden fleece and not one of you would stand against my father
All of you together could not face him
You would have left his kingdom with your tongues cut out so you could tell no one how to find us or your hands cut off so you would never set sail again
Without the secrets I whispered you would have failed every challenge he set you
Without the lies you first whispered to / me

JASON: Say what you need to. I know the triumphs that were won in my name.

MEDEA: In your name
Yes
In name only
Who charmed the snake to get you the fleece?

JASON: Me!

MEDEA: Really?

**JASON**: Yes
You don't have to take my word for it
Ask anyone

**MEDEA**: I did it for you. As you stood trembling behind me. Terrified. The greatest hero of all the ages, and I saved you

**JASON**: Anyone will tell you what your role in my story is

**MEDEA**: I did it for you

**JASON**: When I sailed towards your land a black cloud covered it
When we got closer, I saw that it was a swarm of insects
You cleared the cloud with your darkness
I was young enough then to think that made you the light
I know better now

**MEDEA**: I thought you were the light
You blinded me

**JASON**: Well, no longer
We can each of us move on

**MEDEA**: How?
How?
How Jason?
You made me betray everything I knew and loved because I thought that you loved me
Where can I go?
Jason, you are the only home that is left to me

**JASON**: Whatever you think I have taken from you
Whatever you *think* I have taken from you, you must see what I've given you
Over years
Over years

Yes, you helped me when I needed help, but I think we must both acknowledge now that I helped you more than you ever helped me
Thanks to me you escaped that place
What would you be if you had stayed?
Here you have fame
And fame where it matters
You see I have kept my promise
When I set sail that was all I dreamed of
And I have shared that dream with you and it is the greatest gift that I— that anyone—could give
Your name is spoken
And not only with mine
People know you
Yes
They do
And this new chapter—my marriage
Don't you see?
This is in all of our interests
This marriage is not a denial of my love for you
It is proof of it
Yes
Listen
Proof
What did we come here with?

**MEDEA:**

**JASON:** And what do we have now?
I am married to a princess
Our children will be the brothers of kings
Don't you see?

**MEDEA:** Your children will be kings

**JASON**: Yes. Which will elevate yours. Which will elevate you.

**MEDEA**: You

**JASON**: Yes

**MEDEA**: You

**JASON**: You're jealous

**MEDEA**: No

**JASON**: You need to separate
Prioritise
Think of the boys

**MEDEA**: Ah, so you did this for them?

**JASON**: Yes

**MEDEA**: No
Do you imagine you can come to me now, smelling of her and tell me that you're doing this for my sake?
Surely if any part of this were true, you would have come to me before you married her?

**JASON**: I know you

**MEDEA**: I know you.
Better than I used to.
You didn't do this for me.
You mean you saw me.
Through their eyes.
You saw what being with me made you.
Made our boys

**JASON**: I did this for the boys so yes I did this for you

**MEDEA**: What did we ever ask for except you?

**JASON:** You still have me

**MEDEA:** Where?
Where, Jason, where do we have you?

**JASON:** You chose to do this.
You made it impossible for you to stay
That is on you
Not me

**MEDEA:** What did I do? Did I come to your land uninvited? Did I force my love on you? Did I go straight from your bed to another?

**JASON:** And there it is
That's what all this comes down to for you
This is beneath us
You know what you have done

**MEDEA:**

**JASON:** Look. I came here to offer you support.
To offer what help I can.
If you reject that then I am saddened, but I am not surprised.

**MEDEA:** <u>I want nothing from you</u>

**JASON:** Well, I've done all I can
As I say
You can't help what you are

**MEDEA:** I made you invulnerable. You made me untouchable.

**JASON:** No, Medea. *I* didn't.

*JASON leaves*

*NURSE enters, carrying some kids' things.*

**NURSE:** He's gone then?

**MEDEA:**

**NURSE:** He's gone.
  I spent a lot of my life wishing for love.
  It never looked like this.

**MEDEA:**

**NURSE:** I'll not ever think that what he's done is right.
  Do you hear me?
  I'm not alone in thinking that.
  I know he's not alone [in thinking that he's right]
  I know he's just a man but
  Well, I've never really understood that as an excuse

**MEDEA:**

**NURSE:** I wish his boat had sunk
  There
  I've said it
  Crashed on the rocks before you ever saw him
  Drowned that worthless man

**MEDEA:** I saved his life

**NURSE:** I know you did

**MEDEA:** I saved his life
  My father would have killed him
  I saved his life

**NURSE:** I know

**MEDEA:** And the songs they sing are all about him
  How he beat some mystical army
  How he killed a snake—or a dragon—sometimes it's a dragon
  How he tricked my father
  It was me

Always me
It was me

**NURSE:** You're in there somewhere
In the shadows
They say you're clever
They sing that about you

**MEDEA:** I never cared

**NURSE:** No

**MEDEA:** I never did
I only care now because he does
And now I'll be
Not even a shadow
I am descended from
From sunlight

**NURSE:** Yes

**MEDEA:** And now he would make less than a shadow out of me

*NURSE tries to comfort her. Fails.*

He's a prince wherever he goes and I
I who am descended from kings from gods!
What am I?

They claim him as their own and me, me they [reject]
Into the shadows again
I was not born for this
I was not born to let him do this thing to me

**NURSE:** Where shall we go now?

*A kindness. Perhaps the first. It knocks MEDEA like a blow.*

*Some contact between them—perhaps the NURSE takes MEDEA's hands.*

Where shall we go?

**MEDEA**: There's nowhere

**NURSE**: There must be someone. And if there's someone there's somewhere.
Athens
Aegeus

**MEDEA**: Aegeus

**NURSE**: He swore an oath to you, Medea.

**MEDEA**: Athens

**NURSE**: He came to you a desperate man. That old king. With tears for eyes. Looking to you to help him. Only you.

**MEDEA**: He said he'd been sent a sign. That I would help his wife to conceive.

**NURSE**: A king needs an heir. He said if you helped them he would give you a home, Medea. A home. If ever you had need of one.

**MEDEA**: I do have need of one
    He did have a child
    A son
    You are right
    He swore an oath
    It is more than his own life that he owes to me
    He will not break his vow
    And cannot be made to

**NURSE:** Good
All will be well

**MEDEA:** Yes
All will be as it should be

**NURSE:** You'll be safe there.
More [than that]
Celebrated
A man's not a man without sons
He has no name, no future without them
That's what you've given Aegeus

**MEDEA:** That's what I gave Jason

**NURSE:** Aye, well, Aegeus is old; Jason is young

**MEDEA:** Not as young / as

**NURSE:** For a man.
For a man he is young.
I'm sorry.
I know you don't want to hear it but there it is.
And you've got things to look forward to now.

**MEDEA:** Have I?

**NURSE:** Aye, you have

**MEDEA:** Yes, yes, you're right
I have
Like the light of the flames against the night sky when I set that palace on fire

**NURSE:** Enough of that
Wait until we're far away fae here
Time enough to let it all out then

**MEDEA:** Will you do something for me?

**NURSE:** [Anything]

**MEDEA:** Go to Jason

**NURSE:**

**MEDEA:** If you are my friend you will do this for me
Go to Jason
Tell him
Think of something
Tell him I'm leaving
Tell him I'm ready to go
Tell him it's about the boys
Tell him that, whatever has passed between us, we both only want what is best for them
Tell him that in this we are agreed
Tell him whatever you have to to bring him back here with you
You are right

*NURSE goes*

A man has no future without his sons

*MEDEA paces, thinking, planning.*

**MEDEA:** I am not afraid of the sword but they would see it coming
There would be guards all around and I would be on the ground before I got near enough to
She is not my enemy
His new
Or is she?
What do you say?
A man arrives in your father's land
A land in which you are a princess

In which you can expect every
See—there
There is the root of it
He does not arrive alone
He arrives with a wife
He arrives with children
And yet you look at him and think
What?
Not you—you do not think this—nor I
But she
She only sees the man
I am not flesh to her, my children not blood
And she takes him
And my life—meaning nothing to her—she takes that as well

There is a cloak
A gift from my grandfather
Woven from thread that shines like the sun's rays
They say if you stare at it long enough, the brightness will blind you
They say
And a crown made from the same

These things will be my wedding gift to her
I'll send his sons with these treasures to her—the finest things I own
But the gifts will be for him
They will bring death to his new life
It will be quick but it will not seem it
I know how that feels
I know how that feels

And then he will come running
Having seen his future vanish he'll come back to the only one he has left and find that dead as well
I know
I know
But you know
I cannot leave them
I cannot leave them with him
I cannot

I had a dream last night
His new family, his new friends, his new bride all seated at a table in front of me
Every time I opened my mouth to put my case, to ask for care, for kindness, to show them I am not the things he says about me
They laughed
I thought they were looking at me but they were looking behind me to him
Seated at my back
Their mocking faces an echo of his
If I do not do this they will always be laughing
If I do not do this he will always be laughing at me
And I am not the woman in that dream
Mouth open
Silenced
Mocked
And I will not let him be that man
I will
But only for a moment
When he comes back I'll
I'll
I shall be the wife he wants me to be

I shall be sorry
I shall be
I shall be
*Grateful*
For everything he has done for me
Rescuing me from the only place that has ever held me
Taking me so far from my family that I can never return
Loving me so truly that I knew the oceans were made only for him to sail on them to me
And so what if they're made of my tears?
For what he has given me I will always
Thank him

When I woke from my dream it was because my son was shaking me
He'd been dreaming of dragons
He was racing a dragon and it pulled ahead of him
So to beat it he said he had to grow a new set of wings
And can I do this?
How can I do this thing?
The smell of him
Sleep and sweat and sweetness
And wanting always to be so close so close
So close to me
So sometimes it's more than I can bear

*Enter JASON*

**JASON:** You wanted me

**MEDEA:** I did
I do

**JASON:** What do you want?

**MEDEA:** Your forgiveness

**JASON:**

**MEDEA:** Jason
  Your forgiveness

  You are right
  You were always right
  I speak when I should be silent
  I see that now
  And I am sorry I didn't see it sooner
  I hate myself
  Please
  Please don't hate me
  I spoke only out of love
  I know that sounds
  No, you are right
  I have no right to say that
  I spoke out of jealousy
  I was confused
  I was hurt
  I didn't understand how you could want me and also want her
  But I understand now and I'm sorry
  I do

**JASON:** What do you understand?

**MEDEA:** It was never about want
    Not for you
    It was about necessity
    It was about need

**JASON:** Need?

**MEDEA:** You have raised yourself up and you have made a place for our sons
  I see that now

**JASON:** And for you
    I think only of them
    Since what is best for them is best for all of us

**MEDEA:** / Forgive me

*/ A ball bounces onto the stage. JASON runs after it and off as though chasing after the boys.*

**MEDEA:** Forgive me.

*JASON returns*

**JASON:** You see how happy they are?
    He's asking me when I'm going to teach him to fight again
    I told him he doesn't need lessons—he came into this world fighting
    You remember
    Fists and legs pumping
    You remember
    And I said I fear for my enemies with him around
    I almost pity my enemies having to face the man he'll become
    Why aren't you happy?

**MEDEA:** I am

**JASON:** You're crying

**MEDEA:** I'm happy
    I am
    I am
    I am thinking only of them

**JASON:** Look at me

**MEDEA:** I can't Jason

**JASON**: Look at me

**MEDEA**:

**JASON**: Look at me

**MEDEA**:

**JASON**: I was only ever thinking of you.
I am only ever thinking of you.

**MEDEA**: I know

*A moment.*

**MEDEA**: I am trying to do now as you have
To think only about what is best for them
I know that it is not to be with me

**JASON**: No

**MEDEA**: Think about it
I understand that because of my
There can be no future for me here
No—I am not blaming you
It's a problem of my own making, not one for you to solve but the boys
They shouldn't pay for what I have done
Please
Let them stay with their father
Their place is with you

**JASON**: But Creon

**MEDEA**: Do you think if you asked him, as a father, do you think he might listen to you?

**JASON**: He might

**MEDEA**: Or his daughter
Might he listen to her?

**JASON:** She doesn't know I'm here

**MEDEA:** I have a
 You'll see
 A cloak
 Woven with gold
 Take the boys with this gift for her
 A wedding gift
 From your sons

**JASON:** She doesn't need gifts
 You should hold onto these treasures
 You need them more than she does
 I can buy her a present from them

**MEDEA:** Not like this one
 It was made by my father's father
 Tell her I am sorry I was not more gracious when I had the chance to be
 That I should have honoured her in this way from the start
 Tell her she has nothing to fear from me
 Tell her she is out of my reach and so is her husband
 Tell her / she

**JASON:** I'll ask

**MEDEA:** The gifts are nothing
 The boys are everything

**JASON:** I'll make her understand

**MEDEA:** Give the chest to them to carry to her
  Tell them to kneel
  Tell them to beg her
  Then send them one last time back to me

**JASON:** She will do this for me

**MEDEA:** Go
Go
Go quickly before the boys come out here
Go

*JASON leaves*

**MEDEA:** And when it is done you will send them back to me

*Some time after, MEDEA starts to follow after them. NURSE enters and MEDEA stays.*

**NURSE:** He's taken the boys

**MEDEA:** Good

**NURSE:** I sent the tutor with them
I didn't know what else to do

**MEDEA:** They'll come back

**NURSE:** You know that they are innocents in this
Both of them
You do know that?
Both of you?
They're innocent

**MEDEA:** And what am I?
And what am I?

*NURSE leaves*

There's part of our story that is theirs alone
Where we live happily ever after
Where we live happily
Together

Our eldest son takes a piece of string and ties it around the two of us
Around his parents
We don't stand close
But we stand facing each other
He ties a loop around him
And a loop around me
And again
A figure of eight
I don't know how to break it
Jason steps out of it
And the string falls
Still looped around me
The ties that bind us
They will not break
And my son knows more than his father
In that moment
He knows


When children are born they leave some of their cells behind them
Inside the mother
It is not poetry to say that they are part of me
We do not carry them for nine months
I will carry them inside me forever
It is not a feeling a father can know
Their insides do not alter
They can choose a separateness
To walk the world without this always inside them
Without the mother inside them
Without the child


He has this dark spot above the crease in his right elbow

My baby
My Mermerus
*My first born*
When I run my finger over it I feel it is slightly raised
I always thought that no matter how far or how long he went away from me
In what ways his face would change
That mark beneath my finger would always feel the same
When his hair falls onto his face he tilts his head back and shakes it to push it out of his eyes
Always too busy to use his hands
At night he fights sleep and follows me from room to room telling me he wishes he were an owl
Pheres—my youngest—is a songbird
He'll jump off any surface he can find and never stops talking, asking were you watching did you see me over and over so I have no time to answer and then he pauses: 'why are you laughing at me?'
Never at you, I say, my darling, never at you
'So what's funny?'
He doesn't understand yet that sometimes in laughter there is just joy
That sometimes he is just joy
And my heart is the world and they are the ocean
My love for them never held only inside me but roaring over the edges, eroding the hardened rock I've worked for years to build inside
Washing it into the sea
My love when I hold their hands and look into their faces
And notice how they run differently

It's how I used to watch him

And lie awake in my father's house so afraid so afraid for him
His face, his voice, the way he walked when he left a room
I thought there could be no other man in the world like him
[He turned out to be a man like every other]

*NURSE enters carrying the boys' jackets or some other item of clothes*

**NURSE:** All is well.
I told them to wait in their rooms for you to see them
I can't tell what I thought
You just had a look about you I
I should have
I shouldn't have
It's good news, Medea. They said she loved getting gifts from them and I know—in time — she will grow to love them
What's wrong?
This is what you
I was going to say wanted
Not wanted
Aye, okay but

What you wanted for them

*MEDEA can't breathe*

It's good news.
All will be well.
They're safe.
You've made certain of that.

*MEDEA looks at the audience*

**NURSE:** You're a good mother

**MEDEA:**

**NURSE:** What is it?
What have I said?
I don't mean it's good news for you—I just mean you've done / what's best for them

**MEDEA:** Nothing.
It's nothing you've said.
It's not your fault.
I mean it.
You're not to blame.

**NURSE:** They're yours, Medea.
Nothing can change that.
When they're old enough to have a voice they'll make themselves heard.
I know they'll bring you back one day.

**MEDEA:** No
No
There's no turning back from this

**NURSE:** I know you're in pain and that's all you can see now but it will happen.
This news is good.

**MEDEA:** Yes
Yes
Go now. Get together the things they'll need. Please. I have to say goodbye.

*NURSE leaves.*

**MEDEA:** I have prepared a home for you
Somewhere to hold you
Where no harm will come to you
That's all I ever wanted
I had dreamed other dreams for you
I had imagined that when I grew old you would care enough to care for me
I never could imagine you old
How can I see rough on your faces?
Or scars on your arms
Your hands grown big enough to cover mine
Your hands
But I had thought to watch them grow

They won't let me stay with you
Never
They'll never let me keep you
With me you'll find no peace
Away from you I will have none
I will see you everywhere
Everywhere
And I'll never be able to hold you
No
No
No
Your hands
The way you look up at me
I cannot
No
We're leaving
We're escaping

We're leaving together
I was thinking only of his pain but (*pain—perhaps a cry*)
No
If you leave him it will hurt him but if you leave me I will not survive
No

*She hits herself*

What is wrong with you?
This is what he wants
He is laughing at you
They all are
Just stop stop
They will never stop
Just stop

I cannot do this
I do not have that kind of strength in me
It's not weakness
It's not weak
I will find another way
Athens
We will find a life there
Fool
No
No
What have I done?
They will not stop until they find us
Think
Think now what they will do to them
It's too late
It's too late

I am too late
She's putting the cloak on
She's wearing the crown
She is imagining herself beautiful
She is imagining herself as lovely and as loved as they are
My babies
My boys

I have prepared a home for you
The sun shines day and night so it's never time for bed and there's always time for more
There's always time.
You'll be safe
I promise
The world I've made will be yours

*TUTOR enters*

**TUTOR**: Medea, what have you done?
  Run
  You have to go
  The boys
  You have to run

**MEDEA**: Why?
  Tell me
  Why should I run?

**TUTOR**: They're dead

**MEDEA**: Who's dead?

**TUTOR**: The Princess
  The Princess is dead
  And her father
  Creon

Medea, You've killed the king

**MEDEA:** Both of them?
Dead?
Good

**TUTOR:** You're mad

**MEDEA:** No

**TUTOR:** You killed them

**MEDEA:** I know
Good
Now tell me
Tell me all of it
How long did it take?
How did Creon come to die?

**TUTOR:** Why don't you fear for your life, Medea?

**MEDEA:** My life?
I am a ghost.
Tell. Me. All.

**TUTOR:** When they saw the boys they thought [all will be well]
With Jason
He told us that he'd seen a change in you
And the boys were so happy
We all were

**MEDEA:** Yes, yes and then

**TUTOR:** They presented their gifts to the Princess
Her heart softened
She knelt down to take their hands
To lift them up as they knelt before her
She took Jason's hands

And she promised to love them
As he loved her
She would love them
And he sent them here to kiss you goodbye

**MEDEA:** So fast

**TUTOR:** She turned back to the gifts then
To the cloak
And to the crown

**MEDEA:** Ah, the crown

**TUTOR:** It shone with such a brightness
Not like any gold we'd ever seen

**MEDEA:** Not like gold, no

**TUTOR:** Like the sun

**MEDEA:** Yes.
It was forged in the fire of the sun.
For the descendants of the sun.
It was forged for me.

**TUTOR:** She placed it on her head
And Jason gasped
It was
She was
Radiant

**MEDEA:** And then
The cloak

**TUTOR:** She placed it around her shoulders
The fabric so fine it moulded to her shape as though it was made only for her
She saw herself in the mirror
She saw what we saw

She was always lovely
Beautiful
But now
Now she shone
And she spun
Drawing all the light in the room into her until it seemed as though the only light was from her
As though all light was within her
She turned around and around

**MEDEA**: And then

**TUTOR**: The light still shone from her but
She was reaching
Her arms out but somehow instead of stepping towards her we all
We all stepped away

**MEDEA**: All but one

**TUTOR**: No. Jason, he
He just stood
He just
He just was standing there

**MEDEA**:

**TUTOR**: Slowly what shone from her
It wasn't light
And she was screaming
And Creon
From nowhere
He ran to her
And she sank to the floor
And he followed her
The crown wasn't on her head it was
Her face and the crown they were

Somehow they were the same
And her father he tried to take the cloak from her but her flesh fell off in his hands
He put his hands where her face should have been
He held her head
Rested it on his chest
And howled

**MEDEA:** He howled?

**TUTOR:** Like an animal
A sound I have never heard come from a man
He tried to push her from him
But there was no her to push against just
And the more he fought the more caught up he became and he cried for help / but

**MEDEA:** So he died on his knees

**TUTOR:** I couldn't say
They were all entangled
Flesh and
I cannot say
But they are coming for you
They are afraid
But they are many
Why do you stay here?

**MEDEA:** Why do you?

*He leaves.*

**MEDEA:** You see?
You see?
How many times can this
How many times can Jason stand and watch as those he has sworn to love break?

You are my witness
You know
You know
There is no other way than this

There was only ever one way for him to leave me
There was only ever one way for me to leave him
If we are no more then we never were
If we never were then they
There is no they without us
There can be no more me
There is no other way

The power he has
I'm taking it
I have to
It's mine

*The NURSE comes on. NURSE tries to connect with MEDEA who doesn't respond.*
*MEDEA leaves.*
*NURSE watches her.*
*She looks at the boy's things.*
*She looks after MEDEA.*
*She looks at us.*
*She runs.*
*A silence.*

*MEDEA comes back.*
*She is striding purposefully, holding a bloody dagger or sword.*
*She lets it fall.*
*She's impatient to go now.*
*She's already gone.*

*Just one thing left to do.*

*When the NURSE comes back on stage she is covered in the children's blood.*

*JASON rushes in. He sees the NURSE..*

**JASON:** My boys
Take me to them
There's no time

**NURSE:** She

**JASON:** They will kill them.
Do you understand me?
We have to leave.
Now.

**NURSE:** You're too late

**JASON:** What?
No.
I came here directly

**NURSE:** She took them.
She

*JASON takes the NURSE's hands, the blood now on them both.*

**JASON:** Is that her blood?

**NURSE:** No

**JASON:** No
No

**MEDEA:** Yes

**JASON:** Where are they?

**MEDEA:** She's lying to you, Jason

**JASON:** What?

**MEDEA:** About the blood

**JASON:** Where are they?

**MEDEA:** It is my blood

**JASON:** Yes

**MEDEA:** It is my blood

**JASON:** Good

**MEDEA:** And it is yours

**NURSE:** Listen to her

**MEDEA:** Listen to me

**JASON:** There is no time!

**MEDEA:** It's my blood and it's yours
We mixed them together when we spoke about forever
But forever doesn't exist for us any more now, does it?

**JASON:** No

**MEDEA:** That's what you told me

**JASON:** No

**MEDEA:** Yes

**JASON:**
  I will kill you
  I will kill you

*He won't. She's so far out of his reach.*

**JASON:** You're a monster

**MEDEA:** I am exactly who I have always been
You knew who I was when you chose me
You knew who I was when you threw me away
I am not a part of the story you tried to write
I am the story
And it ends when I say so
Not you
You wanted a monster
Look
You found one
It was always there
It was always with you
You wanted a monster
Look at your hands
You wanted a monster
Look at you now
Look
Love
Look at what you've done

**JASON:** I gave you everything and you
You
You have taken my whole life from me

*MEDEA waits a beat to see if JASON can hear it yet. He can't.*

You will be punished for this

**MEDEA:** Yes
Yes
Yes I will
But not by you
Never by you

**JASON:** Give them to me

**MEDEA:** I will give you what you asked for Jason
I will keep my children with me
We won't get in your way
Go
I believe there are others you should bury

**JASON:** You have no heart

**MEDEA:** Do you feel it?
Now?
Do you?
It's nothing
Not yet
You wait
Wait till you get old
And you will get old
Childless
And old
And one day
When you are praying prayers of desperation
A mast from your ship
The ship you sailed to find fame
Will finally deliver it to you
By falling on your bent head
You'll die on your knees
And that is the only song that will be sung of you
That is all that will remain of your name

**JASON:** Let me see them

**MEDEA:** Why?

**JASON:** I want

**MEDEA:** What?

**JASON:** They are my sons. I want to hold them.

**MEDEA:** They were your sons when you banished them.

**JASON:** Please. / Please. Please

**MEDEA:** You've had enough from me now
I will give you nothing else
Time for change
The sun is rising
And so am I

*MEDEA's gone.*

*JASON remains on stage. He's lost.*

**JASON:** Please
Please

*He's on his knees.*

**NURSE:** There are different stories of what happened that day
Of how she disappeared
This is not that story but I was there so I can tell you what I saw

The sun himself reached down to lift her up
Tore a hole in this world and opened a path to another
The earth she'd stood on scorched with fire
Nothing grows there now
Nothing ever will
This is not a love story
This is not a story of love
She did what she could
And so did I
I can't say I sleep now

No, I can't say that
I'm always there to see when the sun comes up
But she's not one for coming back for those she left behind
She [did what she did]
Enough.


**END**

Nicole Cooper as Medea (photo: by Tommy Ga-Ken Wan)

Isabelle Joss as Nurse (photo: by Tommy Ga-Ken Wan)

## ACKNOWLEDGEMENT

With special thanks to...

Nick Bone, Creative Scotland, Critics Awards for Theatre in Scotland, Lucy George, Catherine King, Emma McKee, Oonagh McKinnon, Linda McLean, Magnetic North Theatre Company, Rona Munro, Lynda Radley, Nicola Stewart, Kirsty Williams, Playwrights' Studio Scotland, Scottish Society of Playwrights.

## RAW MATERIAL

Margaret-Anne O'Donnell and Gillian Garrity co-founded Raw Material, an award-winning, Scottish based independent producing company in 2018.

"Our shared ambition to develop, create and tour bold accessible theatre that inspires, entertains and captivates audience across borders formed the foundations of our company. We are advocates for access and diversity within the sector and are passionate about enabling creative ambition, developing new models for success and supporting all stages of making theatre happen."

Working collaboratively with a wide range of artists, theatre companies, organisations and funders, Raw Material, commission, produce and tour work of varying scale across Scotland, the UK and internationally.

www.rawmaterialsarts.com

# QUESTIONS FOR STUDY AND DISCUSSION

1. What major themes can you identify in the play? What recurring motifs or images are used to convey them?

2. Medea is often treated as both insider and outsider. In what ways is she othered by the society around her, and how does that shape the choices she believes are available to her?

3. What expectations are placed on women in the world of the play? How are those expectations enforced—by individuals, by social customs, or by fear of reputation?

4. Jason justifies his actions in several ways. What arguments does he use to defend himself, and how does the play invite us to test those arguments?

5. At what points do you feel sympathy for Medea, and at what points do you feel disturbed by her? How does the adaptation manage or challenge your allegiance as an audience member?

6. The play repeatedly asks what "justice" means. How do different characters define justice—and whose definition carries power?

7. What role do the community voices, such as the Chorus or group presence, play in this adaptation? Do they function as comfort, judgement, pressure or something else? How do they influence our reading of *Medea*?

8. Identify the key turning points where Medea's plan sharpens or changes. What triggers each shift: emotion, logic, humiliation, fear, or a strategic opportunity?

9. How does McKean's adaptation handle the tension between public image and private truth? Where do characters perform versions of themselves to survive?

10. Consider the theme of exile/home. What does "home" mean to Medea in this version—place, belonging, status, safety, identity? How does losing it intensify the conflict?

11. The play includes persuasion as a kind of power. Which characters persuade successfully, and what techniques do they use?

12. How does this adaptation build tension: through pacing, revelations, repetition, silences, direct address or sudden shifts in tone? Point to moments where you can feel the pressure rising.

13. Medea faces choices with devastating consequences. Which moment do you think is the point of no return—and why that moment, rather than earlier or later?

14. The story is ancient, but it speaks to modern issues. What contemporary situations or headlines does this adaptation make you think about—and what questions does it leave you with?

15. Creative task: choose one scene and rewrite it from another character's perspective—Jason, the community/Chorus, or a confidant. What changes when the story is told by someone with different power, fears and loyalties?

## ALSO AVAILABLE FROM SALAMANDER STREET CLASSICS

All Salamander Street plays can be bought in bulk at a discount for performance or study. Contact info@salamanderstreet.com to enquire about performance licenses.

### HEDDA GABLER by HENRIK IBSEN
### adapted by Kathy McKean
ISBN: 9781919483221

Kathy McKean's new version of Ibsen's ***Hedda Gabler*** crackles with sharp contemporary speech and bruising humour. Returning from honeymoon to a mortgaged house and a stifling marriage, Hedda seethes for agency. Old rivals, failed courage and loaded pistols spiral towards catastrophe, exposing desire, control and fear in a world watching.

### CHATSKY & MISER, MISER!
### translated by Anthony Burgess
ISBN: 9781914228889

Anthony Burgess expertly tackles the major monuments of French and Russian theatre: *The Miser* by Molière and *Chatsky* by Alexander Griboyedov. Burgess's verse and prose plays *Chatsky: The Importance of Being Stupid* and *Miser, Miser!* are published for the first time in this volume.

### LITTLE COMEDIES by ANTON CHEKHOV
### adapted by Richard Nelson
### from translations by Richard Nelson, Richard Pevear, & Larissa Volokhonsky
ISBN: 9781068233494

Five Chekhov one-acts—*The Bear, A Proposal, The Wedding, On the Harmfulness of Tobacco* and *Swan Song*. Farce meets tenderness as lovers quarrel, lectures unravel and an ageing actor faces the empty stage, revealing comedy as a profoundly human condition in the end.

**Salamander Street**

www.ingramcontent.com/pod-product-compliance
Lightning Source LLC
Chambersburg PA
CBHW022119090426
42743CB00008B/919